Apples, Alligators and also Alphabets

To Taylor and Sarah,
and all the other Xoobers
Love,
Mum and Pops

Aa

Apples, Alligators and Also Alphabets

Bb

Bubbles, Balloons and Big Baboons

Cc

Cranes, Caps and Crazy Cats

Dd

Dizzy Dinosaurs and Dancing Doctors

Ee

Elves, Elks and Everything Else

Ff

Flies, Fleas and Furry Feet

Gg

Gulls, Gates, Goats and Grapes

Hh

Hippos, Harps, Hats and Hearts

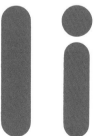

Impish Iguanas, Inchworms and Iris

Jj

Jolly Jokers and Jumping Jackals

Kk

Kangaroo Kings, Keys and Kittens

Ll

Lizards, Loons and Lazy Lagoons

Mm

Monkeys, Moose and Muddy Mice

Nn

Newts, Noodles and Nutty Narwhals

Oceans, Oilskins, Oars and Oysters

Pp

Pink Pigs and Pudgy Pickles

Qq

Queasy Queens and Quantities of Quiche

Rr

Rhinos, Raccoons and Raspberry Rooms

Ss

Sheep Sweeping and Spiders Spinning

Tt

Turtles, Toads and Tickled Tummies

Ww

Weird Walrus and Winking Whales

Xoobers X-ing X-rays with X's

Yellow Yarn and Yodelling Yaks

Zz

Zany Zebras Zapping Z's